# OPERATING

# AND

# THRIVING

# BEHIND ENEMY

# LINES

*A Kingdom Strategy for the Infiltration and Reclaim of the Marketplace.*

**CHARLES OMOLE** LLB, LLM, PHD

Copyright 2017

by Charles Omole


ISBN: 978-1-907095-20-7

Published by:

**WINNING FAITH**
OUTREACH MINISTRIES


*London . New York . Lagos*

# Introduction

Welcome to *"operating behind enemy lines"*.

Firstly, I must state clearly that this book is about one of the many strategies God will use to reclaim the marketplace in these last days.

Operating behind enemy lines is not for everybody. Those chosen for these operations are essential to God's strategic plan. However, the strategy is currently underused and less exploited in the kingdom.

As with under-cover policing, operating behind enemy lines is a complimentary tool available to defeat the enemy. The zeal to declare the glory of our King should be balanced by the need to redemptively impact the mountains and reclaim the marketplace. To achieve this we need effective strategies.

*"When Jesus came to the region of Caesarea Philippi, he asked his disciples, "Who do people say the Son of Man is?" They replied, "Some say John the Baptist; others say Elijah; and still others, Jeremiah or one of the prophets."*

*"But what about you?" he asked. "Who do you say I am?" Simon Peter answered, "You are the Messiah, the Son of the living God." Jesus replied, "Blessed are you, Simon son of Jonah, for this was not revealed to you by flesh and blood, but by my Father in heaven. 18 And I tell you that you are Peter, and on this rock I will build my church, and the gates of Hades will not overcome it. I will give you the keys of the kingdom of heaven; whatever you bind on earth will be bound in heaven, and whatever you loose on earth will be loosed in heaven." Then **he***

***ordered his disciples not to tell anyone*** *that he was the Messiah."* **Matthew 16:13-20**

There are many lessons we can take from this passage of scripture but it is instructive that Jesus in verse 20 ordered his disciples not to tell anyone He was the Messiah. I would have thought He would have told them to go shout it from the mountain tops that He was the Saviour. Now I know the main reason in this instance was the fact that Jesus was yet to be crucified so an un-crucified Christ is not our message. So His instruction is understandable.

In addition, we learn that it is not unusual to know something and still be told to keep it to yourself for a season. Likewise you can hide your identity for a season as part of God's strategic tactic to reclaim the marketplace.

If you go to an Islamic country today, it may be wise not to wear your Christianity  on your sleeve from the airport, as you may not last long in that country that way. So you try to blend in and  make your impact first in discrete ways before you gradually receive wisdom and boldness to reach out to the lost in that nation.

The idea that once you are saved, you should always shout it out loud to the world is a well preached message. But I have come to know that this may not always be the wise path to take if we are to reach the unreached and reclaim the marketplace. There will be many occasions when we will be required to go behind enemy lines and blend in for a season before we unleash our purpose.

The use of the words "Enemy lines" in this book is done with some artistic license. We know the enemy, Satan, is the ruler of the darkness of this world.

So he has a legitimate claim on the earth since Adam gave him the title deed of the earth. And our job is to reclaim it.

Those who already operate in the marketplace frontline will understand this message very easily. It is those who still live in religious bubbles that will find it more difficult and may even see this message as 'compromising' the faith. I have addressed this possible perception in Chapter seven.

Every truth has the potential of creating tension, especially for those who will want to take it to extremes. This is the same tension that exists today in Christianity around the Grace message for example. Some think grace has become an excuse to sin recklessly, but in truth grace empowers us not to sin.

This tension can sometimes be helpful to keep us all in check, but in the end every believer will act in light of the revelation they have received from the Word. There are still believers today who think we should not get involved at all in the marketplace. Others will criticise any message that advocates being active outside of a building called church. These are all grains of thought in the Church, but the counsel of the Lord will always prevail.

Any Biblical truth can be abused. That does not take away from the accuracy of the message. There will be those that will make mistakes as they engage with the marketplace; that does not make our reclaim project any less needed. As more role models are created who are giants in the marketplace, more believers will be able to make the paradigm shifts needed to engage and prosper behind enemy lines.

Beloved, we need to go behind enemy lines, so to speak, to dislodge Satan from all the mountains he currently occupies.

To do this, we will often need to use undercover techniques to penetrate these guarded mountains. This is the focus of this book. Using my own experiences as well as scriptural examples, you will see how we can strategically reclaim the marketplace, being wise as a serpent and gentle as a dove.

The bible says we are being sent out as sheep amongst wolves. To survive, we cannot just look like sheep all the time. We will be easy targets for the wolves. So we may have to blend in with the wolves for a period, gain their confidence and rise to the top in their ranks before we unleash out true purpose. After all, the wolves are expert at coming to us in sheep's clothing. Sometimes, this is not about doing things in a different way, but about not drawing undue attention to yourself in the midst of your enemies. This is wisdom.

To make the kingdoms of this world become the Kingdoms of our God we need to employ all the tools in the box to get it done. So as you read this book, I want you to learn and ask if you are part of the undercover army God will use in these last days. So if you are a believer engaged in Politics, Government, Business, Media, Education, World of Entertainment, Arts and Culture, this book is for you. It will equip you on how to impact your sector for God using unusual wisdom and Kingdom strategies.

Many of the elements of this covert strategy are not suitable for normal friendly environments. They only become essential in hostile or unfriendly territories. As someone who has worked in practically all the countries in the Middle East, I know first hand what it feels like to operate behind enemy lines.

But I want you to be excited about the great future ahead of you, as you take your place in God's end time revival, whether or not your assignment is in undercover operations.

It is shocking that majority of believers do not know the difference between what is culture and what is scripture. Because you have always done something in a particular cultural way does not make it scriptural. It does not mean the way you have always done it is wrong or sinful, but don't equate it to being scriptural either. You criticise others for doing the same thing based on their own culture that is different from yours. Why are many believers so narrow-minded and don't even know it?

From Genesis to Revelation, the Bible did not tell us how to conduct a church service. So a lot of what we do in church is therefore culturally informed. That is not wrong; don't misunderstand me. But it is wrong to then criticise others for conducting service based on their own different culture. We need to separate what is a scriptural dictate from a cultural norm. Mixing the two together is a major cause of needless criticism, conflict and disunity in the Church of Christ.

To reach the lost and take over the marketplace; God will shock many believers with His strategies and instructions. Open your mind to new things from God. Many have spent years trying to correct God, based on their ignorance and shallow mindedness. It is time to move the Kingdom forward.

The Marketplace is a spiritual entity and it will take the spiritually mature in Christ to engage with it successfully. This will require a number of strategies and I believe this book will give you insight into one of them. See you at the top.

Blessings galore.
Dr Charles Omole

# Table of Contents

# CHAPTER ONE

## Be Wise as Serpents and Gentle as Doves

Despair is an easy emotion to embrace given what is going on in our world. Hopelessness and helplessness everywhere you look. Those doing the right things appear to be suffering, while those engaged in all manner of wrong and sinful acts appear to be making it.

In these pervading bleakness, where is God and has He lost control of His cherish creation, the earth?

These are some of the obvious repeated scenarios I face everywhere I go these days. Can God transform the kingdoms of the world to the Kingdoms of His dear son as promised in Revelation 11? How do we as believers operate in the marketplace?

While it is true that there are some that will need to wear the toga of Christianity to fulfil their calling into the Marketplace; for many if not most, their activities in the marketplace will need to be discreet at certain stages, only revealing their true status at the appointed time. In every generation, God will not leave himself without a witness.

So amongst the despair that we see, God has His secret agents operating under cover and to the casual mind, they are just like the unbelievers. These are the first group of people this book is primarily directed at. Those who will operate behind the scene in Babylon, rise through the ranks to the top of the mountains before unleashing the God agenda they have been incubating all along.

This book is also for every believer, who needs to understand the operations of God on the earth by developing divine wisdom in dealing with people of diverse assignments.

Could people we see daily in different sectors that appear ungodly in fact be God's secret Agents in the marketplace? Could people we condemn be those doing what is needed to maintain their cover in the enemy's territories?

This is why we all need to be discerning and not just criticise people for actions needed to protect their undercover operations. We all need to accept that God has a settled strategy to reclaim the earth and all we need to do is tune to heaven's frequency to hear from the Master.

So over the past few years, I picked up that Christians are despairing. Reading the news, you see what's happening:

Christians are being persecuted and even killed endlessly in the Middle East. Some people are saying that the tribulation has started which is not true. If you know your Bible, you know that what's happening now is nothing compared to the tribulation that is to come.

Some believers are also looking to governments for help but that is not forthcoming as they (the politicians) are equally confused about what solution will fix their economies. But you need to understand that God is still in charge and He has a strategy, which many of us may not fully understand yet.

The Bible states that we should put on the whole armour of God. But if you read scriptures, you will see that there is no armour for your back. Everywhere else is covered, except the back.

We are supposed to thrive in relationships and our companions in this journey of life are supposed to rally and have our back. For instance, if asked, who killed Uriah? What will you say? David? That's not true.

David did not kill Uriah because all David simply said was to *put him at the forefront of the hottest battle.* That's not what killed Uriah. In fact, *'put him at the forefront of the hottest battle'* is like telling a professional driver 'go and drive a Ferrari'.

That is what Uriah a mighty warrior lived for, so that didn't kill him. What killed Uriah was evident in the second instruction that David gave. He said put him at the forefront of the hottest battle and *withdraw the valiant men from him.* Uriah was fighting alone, nobody had his back. That's what killed him. The withdrawal of other fighters from him. He was fighting with no protection or cover for his back.

So it is important to know that we need relationships and it is absolutely key to be connected to the right people. In this book, I want to show you through scriptures that maybe you and definitely others you know will have an assignment to the marketplace that requires you to work under cover until the "reveal" time comes. 'So I will be examining how to operate behind enemy lines in the marketplace.

From the book of Genesis, we understand that the title deed of the earth was given to Adam (Mankind) and then Adam passed it on to Satan. Hence Satan became the ruler of the darkness of this world, thus giving him unfettered access to the earth. So everything on earth is now within the control of Satan.

That's why if you look at the third temptation of Christ, the Bible says that Satan took Jesus to the top of a mountain and said 'look at the whole world' and showed him the world and its glory. Satan told Jesus, *'bow down to me, I will give it to you for it was delivered unto me'*.

What that means is that Satan is the legitimate ruler of the darkness of this world. Hence, for us as believers, technically operating on earth is tantamount to operating behind enemy lines.

To understand how this works, we need to understand some of the ways of operation of special forces when they infiltrate an enemy's camp or spies go undercover in hostile territories. They must blend in and maintain their cover until it is time to make the final push. How do we operate on earth as currently constituted which is technically an enemy territory?

The special forces blend in with their environment while maintaining focus on their assignment. But to do that, they have to work to predetermined strategies, while improvising along the way; and many times that's what we are lacking in the church.

From time to time, people ask: where are the Daniels, the Josephs, where are the Esther's of our day?

- Where is the power of Godly purpose seen in Joseph?
- Where is the power of consecration we read about in Daniel who refused to be polluted by Babylon?
- Where is the power of focus we see in the apostle Paul who refused to give up in the face of opposition?

Why has the power of God seemed so undermined in many nations? But folks, don't despair, God has a strategy.

To reclaim the marketplace, we must connect with His strategy and with His methods. We must develop the spirit and the skill to live, operate and function behind enemy lines.

Enemy territory is not a place soldiers go to willingly or lightly. It is a product of necessity, a crucial strategy needed to win a war. You don't send your soldiers behind enemy lines if it is not a vital tool or strategy you need to win a war because it is a dangerous thing to do.

Many Christians have used the words Battle, Warfare and fight to describe the race we are in. But most have not fully realised that battles require strategies and tactics, both spiritual and physical.

But when soldiers are sent behind enemy lines it is usually as part of a strategy to neutralise enemies. In many old war movies, you see covert agents being sent behind enemy lines to gather intelligence or plant explosives or even get close to the top hierarchy and neutralise them.

If you read any book on war strategies, you will notice that a salient tactic of operating behind enemy lines is the ability to blend with the enemy until it is time to take action.

For that season, you will be required to live like the enemy, behave like them but knowing there are some lines you may not be able to cross. God can save by the many and He can save by the few. He has many strategies at His disposal. The trouble is that many believers have boxed God into a single strategy and discounted all others.

As a result, many believe they must always tattoo *"Saved"* on their foreheads when engaging with the marketplace. Their *"I am a Born Again Christian"* banner is seen from a mile away before they get to the target.

While it is true some will need to wear a toga of Christianity to fulfil their mandate in the marketplace; it is also true that many are destined to work behind enemy lines for a season, pretend to be part of them and rise to the top of the mountains to cut off the heads of the principalities so to speak.

This adaptive skill is grossly lacking in the Church. Many believers lack the ability to engage and deal with people of diverse temperament. The Bible says we should be as wise as serpent and gentle as dove.[1] These are two opposite and contrasting personalities and characteristics we are being asked to possess.

In sending out the Twelve, Jesus said to them, *"Behold, I send you forth as sheep in the midst of wolves: be ye therefore wise as serpents, and harmless as doves"* (Matthew 10:16, KJV). The NIV Bible says, *"shrewd as snakes and as innocent as doves."*

---

[1] Matthew 10:16

Jesus was using similes (figures of speech that compare two dissimilar things) to instruct His disciples in how to behave in their ministry. Just before He tells them to be wise as serpents and harmless as doves, He warns them that they were being sent out *"like sheep among wolves."*

The world then, as now, was hostile to believers—not incidentally hostile, but purposefully hostile. Wolves are intentional about the harm they inflict upon sheep. In such an environment, the question becomes *"how can we advance the kingdom of God effectively without becoming prey ourselves?"* Jesus taught His followers that, to be Christ-like in a godless world, they must combine the wisdom of the serpent with the harmlessness of the dove. But will a wise shepherd send his precious sheep deliberately amongst wolves? What will wolves do to sheep? Surely, the only reason a loving shepherd will send his sheep into the camp of wolves will be because he has a strategy in place that will protect them. This strategy will either keep them as sheep while incapacitating the wolves or make them appear like wolves even though they are sheep beneath the disguise. The truth is, God can use both strategies and more. But one thing common to all these strategies will be the need for us to adapt.

This adaptive strategy is also what Apostle Paul meant when he stated that he became all things to all men so that he could win some.[2] Being all things to all men require a high level of adaptive skill to blend with diverse groups and cultures.

In using these similes in the book of Matthew, Jesus invokes the common proverbial view of serpents and doves. The serpent was "subtle" or "crafty" or "shrewd" in Genesis 3:1.

---

[2] 1 Corinthians 9:19-23

The dove, on the other hand, was thought of as innocent and harmless—doves were listed among the "clean animals" and were used for sacrifices.[3] To this very day, doves are used as symbols of peace, and snakes are thought of as "sneaky."

A Nineteenth-century pastor, Charles Simeon provides a wonderful comment on the serpent and dove imagery: *"Now the wisdom of the one and the harmlessness of the other are very desirable to be combined in the Christian character; because it is by such an union only that the Christian will be enabled to cope successfully with his more powerful enemies".[4]*

There are certain jobs you may never get if you wear Christianity on your forehead. There are certain nations you may never enter if you put on a toga of

---

[3] Leviticus 14:22
[4] Horae Homileticae: Matthew, Vol. 11, London: Holdsworth and Ball, p. 318

Christianity. There are certain sectors you may never have access to unless you somewhat blend in.

God is sending us as sheep amongst wolves;[5] so we have to learn to behave and look like wolves for a season, so that we can conduct our undercover operation successfully and before the wolves realise what is going on, we would have completed our mission.

Most people don't mind having their character compared to a dove's purity and innocence. But some people recoil at the image of a serpent, no matter what the context. They can never see a snake in a good light, even when used by Jesus as a teaching tool.

But we should not make too much of the simile. We cannot attach the evil actions of Satan (as the serpent) with the serpent itself. Animals are not moral entities.

---

[5] Matthew 10:16

The creature itself cannot perform sin, and shrewdness is an asset, not a defect. This is the quality that Jesus told His disciples to model.

The serpent simile stands in Jesus' dialogue without bringing forward any of the serpent's pejoratives. It is a basic understanding in language that, when a speaker creates a simile, he is not necessarily invoking the entire potential of the words he has chosen—nor is he invoking the entire history and tenor of the linguistic vehicle.

Rather, the speaker is defining a fresh relationship between the two things. A quick look at Matthew 10:16 shows that Jesus was invoking only the positive aspects of the serpent.

There is no hint of His unloading Edenic baggage upon His disciples. He simply tells them to be wise (and innocent) as they represented Him.[6]

When Jesus told the Twelve to be as wise as serpents and harmless as doves, He laid down a general principle about the technique of kingdom work. As we take the gospel to a hostile world, we must be wise (avoiding the snares set for us), and we must be innocent (serving the Lord blamelessly).

Jesus was not suggesting that we stoop to deception but that we should model some of the serpent's famous shrewdness in a positive way. Wisdom does not equal dishonesty, and innocence does not equal gullibility.

In Matthew 10:16, Jesus taught us how to optimize our gospel-spreading opportunities. Successful Christian living requires that we strike the optimal balance between the dove and the

---

[6] https://gotquestions.org/wise-serpents-harmless-doves.html

serpent. We should strive to be gentle without being pushovers, and we must be sacrificial without being taken advantage of.

So my mission in this book is to show you that we must be strategic in our approach to the marketplace. This wisdom is also seen in the Bible in the story of Samuel.

When God told Samuel to go to the house of Jesse to anoint a new king for Israel. God said; *"How long will you mourn for Saul, seeing I have rejected him from reigning over Israel? Fill your horn with oil, and go; I am sending you to Jesse the Bethlehemite. For I have provided Myself a king among his sons."*[7]

Samuel replied that it would be a dangerous move for him because king Saul would kill him if he ever found out his true mission. What did God say?

---

[7] 1 Samuel 16:1

But the Lord said, *"Take a heifer with you, and say, 'I have come to sacrifice to the Lord.' Then invite Jesse to the sacrifice, and I will show you what you shall do; you shall anoint for Me the one I name to you."*[8]

So we can see how God used the heifer as a decoy to hide Samuel's true mission. This is another example of how to be as wise as serpent when operating behind enemy lines.

There are certain countries and cities that you will not be able to enter today if you wear your Christianity as a neck chain. But how do we reach the folks living there with the gospel, unless we use wisdom to go behind enemy lines.

So we need to understand the need to be skilled in operating behind the enemy lines. Sadly, some believers if sent

---

[8] 1 Samuel 16:2-3

behind the enemy lines will be caught almost immediately.

They will not stay under cover long enough to make any impact. They will so stand out and out of place; they will fail in their mission to reclaim the mountains for the Lord.

You need to understand that operating behind enemy lines, requires certain skills that we will be looking at in this book. Like I stated before, the tactics in this book will not be for every believer.

But if you know you  have been sent to reclaim the kingdoms of this world to become the kingdoms of our God and His Christ, then you need the knowledge contained in this book to allow you to stay in character while under cover but still maintaining your right standing with God.

The rules of warfare change once you are behind enemy lines. We need to be skilled in being as wise as serpents and gentle as doves.

# CHAPTER TWO

## Scriptural examples of Covert Operatives

In high level covert operations run by groups like the CIA,[9] once you are behind the enemy lines the rules change. Hence if you are caught and killed it will not be publicised.

In fact in some extreme operations, the United States government will deny any knowledge of who you are. The government that sent you will say they don't know anything about you. It's that serious; so the rules change once you are behind enemy lines.

---

[9] Central Intelligence Agency (CIA) is an American external secret service agency.

In covert operations training, the first cardinal rule you are taught is to *never get caught*. We need to understand, we are operating as believers in the world which is under the control of the Ruler of the darkness of the world, Satan himself.[10]

The Bible says we are in the world but we are not of the world.[11] So when we are operating behind enemy lines there are certain rules that we must be aware of because in the enemy territory the enemy is in charge. The enemy makes the rules, not you, not me. We are in enemy territory.

Satan is the ruler of this world, so just like special forces are equipped to infiltrate and win behind enemy lines, God has also equipped his Church to

---

[10] John 12:31; 16:11; 1 John 5:19
[11] John 17:14-15

overcome in this enemy territory. Thus reclaiming it for God.

I will now like to take you through some scriptural examples. I will give scriptural instances before I give the strategies on prospering behind enemy line.

*Joseph, the secret disciple*

The first example I will like to give you is in John chapter 19. Joseph of Arimathea, who the Bible says in verse 38 of John chapter 19, was a follower of Jesus acted *in secret.* In other words, he would play to the gallery when Jesus' detractors discussed their hatred for Him but he had a different agenda in mind from them. I am sure so much so that when the Pharisees were abusing Jesus he may not have defended his master openly so as not to blow his cover.

Joseph was actually a part of the Council, or Sanhedrin—the group of Jewish religious leaders who called for

Jesus' crucifixion. He must have truly blended in, deep under cover.

However, as we read in scriptures, we see that Joseph was not only opposed to the Council's decision and was, in fact, a secret follower of Jesus.[12] Joseph was a wealthy man.[13] In addition, the Bible refers to Joseph as a *"good and upright man."*[14]

The Bible says he was a secret follower of Jesus. But why did he act secretly? Why did Nicodemus come to Jesus at night? Why not during the day? We see in John 19, how Joseph and Nicodemus acted to give Jesus a befitting burial.

*Afterwards Joseph of Arimathea, who had been a **secret disciple of Jesus** for fear of the Jewish leaders, boldly asked Pilate for permission to take Jesus' body down; and Pilate told him to go ahead. So*

---

[12] See also Mark 15:43
[13] Matthew 27:57
[14] Luke 23:50

*he came and took it away. Nicodemus, the man who had come to Jesus at night, came too, bringing a hundred pounds of embalming ointment made from myrrh and aloes. Together they wrapped Jesus' body in a long linen cloth saturated with the spices, as is the Jewish custom of burial.*[15]

So you need to understand that Joseph of Arimathea became a vital tool to fulfil scripture because it had been prophesied by the prophets that He would be in a tomb,[16] not in a mass grave.

Who was God going to use to make that happen? It's got to be somebody that had enough clout to go to Pilate.

It had to be somebody higher up in the echelon of the system, that have that stature to approach Pilate to demand for

---

[15] John 19:38-42 (TLB)
[16] Isaiah 53:9

the body of Jesus, not some lowly
follower.

After Jesus' death on the cross, Joseph,
at great risk to himself (of blowing his
cover) went to the Roman governor Pilate
to request Jesus' body. Nicodemus, the
Pharisee who had visited Jesus at night[17]
to ask questions about God's Kingdom,
accompanied Joseph.

The two men were granted custody of
Jesus' body, and they immediately began
to prepare the body for burial.

So Joseph and Nicodemus hurriedly
placed Jesus in Joseph's own tomb,
located in a garden near the place of
Jesus' crucifixion.

Unbeknownst to Joseph and Nicodemus,
their choice to put Jesus in Joseph's
tomb fulfilled Isaiah's prophecy spoken
hundreds of years before Jesus' death:

---

[17] John 19:39

*"He was assigned a grave with the wicked, and with the rich in his death, though he had done no violence, nor was any deceit in his mouth."*[18] This is one of the many prophecies that have confirmed Jesus' identity as the Messiah and Son of God.

So it's important to recognise that Joseph's passion for Jesus needed to be in secret to allow him to rise through the ranks in the council, to enable him develop the clout and access needed to influence Pilate.

So if you had seen Joseph with the rest of the council members, you would have concluded he was an enemy of Jesus too. But he was operating behind enemy lines, revealing himself only when it became necessary to accomplish his mission of fulfilling the prophecy of Isaiah.

---

[18] Isaiah 53:9

*Hebrews in the Philistine camp.*
Another example of covert operatives in strategic battle victory is in 1 Samuel Chapter 14.

*Now it happened one day that Jonathan the son of Saul said to the young man who bore his armor, "Come, let us go over to the Philistines' garrison that is on the other side." But he did not tell his father. And Saul was sitting in the outskirts of Gibeah under a pomegranate tree which is in Migron.*

*The people who were with him were about six hundred men. Ahijah the son of Ahitub, Ichabod's brother, the son of Phinehas, the son of Eli, the Lord's priest in Shiloh, was wearing an ephod. But the people did not know that Jonathan had gone.*

*Between the passes, by which Jonathan sought to go over to the Philistines' garrison, there was a sharp rock on one side and a sharp rock on the other side. And the name of one was Bozez, and the name of the other Seneh. The front of one faced northward opposite Michmash, and the other southward opposite Gibeah.*

*Then Jonathan said to the young man who bore his armor, "Come, let us go over to the garrison of these uncircumcised; it may be that the Lord will work for us. For nothing restrains the Lord from saving by many or by few."*

*So his armorbearer said to him, "Do all that is in your heart. Go then; here I am with you, according to your heart."*

*Then Jonathan said, "Very well, let us cross over to these men, and we will show ourselves to them. If they say thus to us, 'Wait until we come to you,' then we will stand still in our place and not go up to them. But if they say thus, 'Come up to us,' then we will go up. For the Lord has delivered them into our hand, and this will be a sign to us."*

You know, most of us want God to look like somebody we personally admire based on our own taste. Who you admire is your own taste.

God is the God of all flesh, so even those with tattoos, He is their God too. Somebody comes to your church and he has tattoos; many will freak out and call him Satan. We need to understand that God is the God of ALL FLESH. That includes people who do not look like you or dress like you.

What does a Christian look like? What happens when somebody got tattoos all over their body and then got saved tomorrow. Suddenly, do you want them to wipe off all the tattoos by magic? Or for him to use his tattoo and connect with all the other people who have tattoos who are not saved.

So in this passage of the Bible; the Philistines were a strong army and the entire army of Israel was in a cave hiding because they were afraid for their lives.

It got to the point Johnathan said 'I am tired of hiding' so Johnathan and his armour bearer, the Bible says, crept out of the cave at night without letting the rest of the crew know.

The Bible says that as he was climbing God stepped in, He brought confusion to the army of the Philistines but that's not the full story of how they won the battle.

The way they won the battle was that God activated a silent cell of Hebrews who had been living amongst the Philistines all along. So for all the weeks the Philistines were harassing the children of Israel (the Hebrews) there were Hebrews in their camp who blended in but did nothing.

The moment Jonathan took that step of faith and then confusion set in, the Hebrews arose who had been silent within the Philistine all these while. Philistines were now not fighting just an external enemy, they were fighting internal ones too.

*Moreover the **Hebrews that were with the Philistines before** that time, which went up with them into the camp from the country round about, even they also turned to be with the Israelites that were with Saul and Jonathan.*[19]

So we can see how the Hebrews operated behind enemy lines for weeks. They worked and served and trained with the Philistines. They earned their confidence.

They hid their true allegiance until it was time to break cover. The Philistines must have by now trusted them and relied on

---

[19] 1 Samuel 14:21

their loyalty to their detriment, they found out.

So for a season God allowed the Hebrews to blend in. There are Christians in governments of nations today who have been working and operating deep behind enemy lines, waiting for the time to reveal themselves.

That is why I stated earlier that you should not despair at happenings on the earth. God is still in full control. He still has thousands that have not bowed their knees to Baal. He has his secret witnesses on every mountain of culture.

But God needs more secret agents on every mountain. People who will be so schooled and skilled in the ways of Egypt that they will know how to readily dismantle the systems of Babylon.

You must understand that if God has called you to reclaim the marketplace, you may need to learn how to blend in while still retaining your focus on God's agenda.

That's what the apostle Paul meant, when he said, *"to the Jews, I became a Jew, to those without the law I became as though without the law, even though I am under the law of Christ...I became all things to all men that I may win some."*

In other words, if you see me on Monday with the Jews, I will dress the way they dress, everything they don't eat I won't eat. I will be a good Jew. See me on Wednesday with those without the law, I will eat everything they eat, I will dress the way they dress. He was blending in with the different groups and cultures so that he would not stand out in a negative way.

This is not an invitation to lawlessness. Paul emphasised that he was always under the law of Christ. So this is not about committing sin in the name of blending in. No. It is about using people's culture and understanding to relate with them rather than shoving only your views down their throat.

Paul explains that he is always under the law of Christ and is never free to do things that would be contrary to the new covenant. And in Galatians 5:13 he says, *"For, brethren, ye have been called unto liberty; ONLY USE NOT LIBERTY FOR AN OCCASION TO THE FLESH, but by love serve one another."*

Paul's liberty in his evangelism was not a freedom to serve the flesh in any way. Paul was always strict in regard to sin and he did not allow anything in his life that would bring the result of sin by spiritual carelessness.

He would not become a glutton to reach other overeaters; he would not become a drug user to reach the addict; he would not become a drinker of alcohol to reach a drunk.

And in 1 Corinthians 9:27 Paul says, *"But I discipline my body and BRING IT INTO SUBJECTION: lest that by any means, when I have preached to others, I myself should become disqualified (a castaway)"*

Paul simply meant that he would use their own beliefs and ways to show them the truth. So to a religious Jew, he would use the law to speak to them; to a Gentile, he would use his conscience and culture.

In fact in legitimate undercover operations (not talking about the CIA type dodgy operations); there are certain lines you are not allowed to cross.

This is because criminal prosecution is always the end game of many undercover operatives. And you will fail in court if the undercover agent has recklessly broken the law in the process of gathering intelligence and evidence.

You are also not allowed to induce crime when under cover. That means you are not allowed to make people commit a crime they would not otherwise have committed. This is the principle of Agent Provocateur in English law.

Agent provocateur has been defined as a person who entices another to commit an express breach of the law which they would not otherwise have committed and then proceeds to inform against them in respect of such an offence.

British case law has established that conduct by undercover agents which does no more than present the subject(s) of the operation with an unexceptional opportunity to commit a crime which they would have committed with another is perfectly acceptable.[20]

However, the undercover agent must not instigate the commission of a crime which would not otherwise have been committed with somebody else.

So even in the natural, you are not allowed to do whatever you wish while under cover, how much more in the spiritual race we are in. Hence, working under cover is about understanding the enemy, knowing their weaknesses and how you can legitimately exploit it, without breaching the law yourself.

As we look at some detailed strategies later, you will see that sometimes simply keeping silent is enough for you to blend in. It's not always about doing the wrong thing; but about making yourself unseen and not standing out to allow you infiltrate the enemy more deeply. But it

[20] R v Loosely [2001] UKHL 53

will require flexibility and adaptiveness that many Christians seem not to have these days.

Apostle Paul said we should be all things to all men, but we are one thing to all men. This is not wise. So you adapt your skill, adapt your temperament, adapt your language to suit the environment you are in. It's absolutely key because if they don't assume you are one of them, your undercover operation will fail from the start.

## A Personal example

A long time ago (more than twenty years), I was part of a major national political campaign in Nigeria. I was in the strategy division. I actually produced a document that analysed the political campaign strategy in every one the States in Nigeria and what tactics were needed to win in each state.

One of the things that characterise political meetings in Nigeria, is the late night nature of the meetings. But I noticed after we visited the second state that the protocol team would have arranged girls (prostitutes will be best used to describe them) for each one of us strategic team member (who were all men) as part of the evening 'entertainment'.

So I was in a bind as to what to do. I wanted to maintain my position under cover so as to see how far I could rise on that mountain but did not wish to commit to that lifestyle. This was when God began to show me what it takes to operate successfully behind enemy lines.

So I sought wisdom from God. The usual process was that as we arrived in a state in the afternoon, the protocol head would give us our room keys. We would then go for an early dinner. At the table would be girls already briefed and ready for you.

You then take yours to your room and then come down at about 11pm to start the meetings. You go back to your room again early in the morning and come down finally for breakfast later. The team then moved to another state. That was the pattern from state to state.

I immediately asked God for wisdom and He told me what to do. I was granted favour. I spoke to the head of protocol that I would need an additional room in every state we went. He assumed I wanted the room for a secret friend, but I did not correct his assumption. He gladly obliged. So as we arrived the hotels in each state, he would give me keys to two rooms.

As we arrived at dinner all the ladies were there, and everyone got his own. After dinner, everybody dispersed till the 11pm meeting. As I got to my floor, I pretended I was unwell to the girl and gave her the key to the additional room and also some money. In the morning we walked down together to breakfast and blended in with the rest of the crew.

That was how I travelled all the states, maintaining my integrity before God, but remaining deeply embedded behind enemy lines. This assignment allowed me extensive contacts in the political class which still yields access to power till today.

But is that not compromise someone could ask? My own question is what did I compromise? Was it my job to lecture these political heavyweights about morality?

So what would have happened if I had declared to the folks that what they were doing was sinful and wrong, preached at them and so on. Such moral high ground posture (in that environment) would make them uncomfortable and my membership of the campaign inner circle would have been short lived. Thus access withdrawn.

Today, several members of that campaign group are born again believers. That is why we need to be as wise as serpents and gentle as doves.

As we operate in the marketplace, there will be many times that we need to be smart and discreet but not compromise. We need to learn the skill that you don't always show your full cards until it's necessary to do so. Hope this example make good sense to you.

So you need to learn that sometimes you have to win their confidence in the marketplace. Have you seen movies where cops are sent undercover into criminal gangs? The undercover cops often have to learn to speak the language of the gangs so as to blend in.

Otherwise, they wouldn't get close to that gang boss they were sent to take out. Sometimes you blend in to bleed them out. This is not compromise. It is called wisdom. But this approach will not be for everybody, just like working undercover is not for every police officer.

A significant challenge is the way many believers are quick to judge others without considering the full story. Lack of discernment means most in the Church judge purely by the seeing of their eyes and logic. They do not allow God to inform them and lead them to a more accurate interpretation of what they see.

Imagine if somebody had seen me with those politicians; everybody with girlfriends. It would have been easy to conclude that I was a player like the rest of them. That is why one of the characteristics you need for a successful engagement and operation in the marketplace is that you must develop a *crowd resistance mentality*.

It is too common to see believers criticising what they do not understand. Consider if Abraham had confided in someone while on his way to sacrifice his son but that person later saw both of them walking the street a week later.

It is very certain the friend would conclude that Abraham was a liar and fraud since Isaac was still alive. But that would be wrong as the friend would not have been privy to what took place on the mountain top between Abraham and God.

This is why I am very hesitant to condemn others for actions that may appear wrong unless I get a spiritual insight into their reasoning or have personal access to them to discuss the situation. What you see can be misleading.

The Bible says if our hearts condemn us not, then we have confidence with God.[21] You have got to get to the point where the matter is between you and God and don't care what anybody else thinks, because the moment you seek to please people, you will blow your cover. And once your cover is blown, that's it.

*Mordechai and Esther hid their Identity*
Another biblical example is Mordechai and Esther, a well-known story. They hid their identity as Jews for a season so that they could thrive and rise to the top behind enemy lines.

They hid their identity until the right time to reveal their identity came. Now folks, their hiding their identity was not just a product of words, they must have changed their mannerism, their tone and everything because it's one thing to deny being a Jew, it's another thing not to dress like a Jew. Do you understand?

---

[21] 1 John 3:21

Esther and Mordecai must have blended in behind enemy lines to successfully fool the king and hide their Jewish identity. That is the kind of skill we need to operate behind enemy lines. In the same vein, Daniel did a deal to keep himself from eating the king's portion.

Developing the essential skills to successfully operate behind enemy lines is critical to our marketplace reclaim strategy.

Because if we don't know and learn how to operate successfully behind enemy lines, we will always be sent away from the foot of every mountain of culture; we'll never get to the top of it.

If we don't learn these strategies, we will always remain at the foot of the mountain and they'll shut us out.

To get to the top will mean blending in with the enemy for a period. That's what the apostle Paul meant when he said, *'to the Jew , I am a Jew..."*

Clearly, we know  there will be some red line which we cannot cross as we are under the law of Christ. But  until we get to that line, we should blend along.

# CHAPTER THREE

## Practical Competencies of Operatives Behind Enemy Lines

While not fully the same as the well established undercover procedures used by security forces globally, there are some competencies believers must possess to operate and prosper on earth while reclaiming the marketplace.

To operate behind enemy lines, you need certain competencies that will enable you to survive in the enemy territories. As you will be moving between what you will normally do and what you will need to do in the peculiar circumstances you will encounter while under cover, you need high-level broad skills and creativity.

Throughout much of church history, people have been stripped of their God-given gifts, talents, and desires, under the guise of devotion and consecration to Christ. This stripped-down version of Christianity removes the believer from ministry, and relegates that privilege to a certain class of Christians called "ministers."

The regular believer's role is reduced to mere financial and emotional support of those in public ministry. And of course to serve as workers in the "local church".

The honour of service and giving to promote ministry must not be devalued, but its emphasis should never be at the expense of each individual carrying their own creative expression of the Gospel through realising their God-given dreams and desires. This is the Kingdom paradigm needed to reclaim the marketplace.

Certain skills are universally accepted as core competencies which underpin your ability to operate behind enemy lines.

These are:
a)  Social skills (social intelligence)

b)  Communication skills

c)  Commitment and drive (motivation)

d)  Resilience and confidence

e)  Self and team development

f)  Professionalism (including integrity)

g)  Undercover credibility

h)  Creative planning

i)  Dynamic decision-making

j)  Effective evidence and administration

k)  Knowledge, research and preparation

*Social skills (social intelligence)*

Ability to get along with people of diverse culture and temperaments is required if you are to prosper in your undercover operation. You must become a people person.

You must be friendly and love meeting people. You must also be astute about the sensitivities of diverse cultures and be able to get along with people even if you do not like what they stand for.

## Communication skills

Communication is an essential skill and competency. You have to be able to get your message across in ways that can be understood by people of diverse perspectives.

One of the main rules of communication is that you have not communicated until you have been understood. Simply saying something does not mean you have been understood. Hence you will need to be able to use various tools and channels to communicate. You also have to be a good listener and able to be trusted.

You have to make people relax around you and feel comfortable speaking to you. That is how you gather vital intelligence.

You will also need to be good with the use of technology and social media. You cannot communicate in the 21st Century without technology skills and social media awareness.

*Commitment and drive (motivation)*
To operate behind enemy lines you will have to be able to endure long periods alone. You will spend time with people you may not necessarily like.

You need to be motivated and committed to the course. You must be driven and committed to the journey, otherwise, you may unwittingly break your own cover. The length of time it may take to complete your undercover operation may be longer than you anticipated. You must be able to endure till the end.

*Resilience and confidence*
As you will see in the next chapter,

confidence is a vital key to surviving under cover. You will need deep resilience to adapt and you need to become flexible.

Resilience means whatever is thrown at you, you find a creative solution that keeps your undercover status intact.

*Self and team development*
You have to become expert at constantly adding value to yourself. Continuous professional development must be your passion. You must know how to develop your skills and become better at what you do.

Given that you will be working with others in the marketplace (people with differing agenda), you have to learn how to work as part of a team.

*Professionalism (including integrity)*
Sounds ironic but to operate under cover successfully, you need strong moral anchors. You must have a strongly held

belief system that will stand the test of the pressure you will come under. Otherwise, you will break easily and lose yourself in the mess you will inevitably encounter while under cover.

So for you to thrive behind enemy lines, you need to have a strong bible-based belief system and Integrity that will enable you resist the baits of the enemy.

In addition to faith to receive from God, you also need to develop the **faith to refuse from Satan.** The Bible says in Hebrews that Moses developed the faith to refuse.[22] That was the reason he could turn his back on Egypt and identify with slaves. You will not need faith to refuse if what you are refusing is a bad thing.

You need it because the enemy will dangle before you the juiciest offers and you will need all the strength you have in your spirit-man to refuse it. The enemy

---

[22] Hebrews 11:24

knows how to corrupt through baits and temptations.

You also need to be professional in your work ethic. One of the challenges with many believers in these last days is the sloppy and carefree attitude many have towards business.

The greatest problems I have had in business have been with so-called Christians. But while working undercover with unbelievers, you will not last five minutes if you are not professional in your approach to work. This will blow your cover and deny you access needed to rise with your chosen mountain of influence.

*Undercover credibility*
If you are a new weightlifter, you don't start by lifting the 200kg weight on your first day. You will injure yourself that way. You start my lifting 20kg and then progress from there. Same with working behind enemy lines. You need to build

your credibility through small assignments first.

You need to start from the position on the mountain that corresponds with your ability and then rise from there. You don't try to enter an industry as Chief Executive Officer if you are a junior staff. You start at a lower level and move your way up over time.

This allows you to build credibility that convinces both you and the enemy. Undercover credibility is crucial. You must not despise the days of small beginnings because as the Bible states, even though your beginning may be small...your latter days will greatly increase.[23]

So don't try to punch above your weight to start with. Start with a level that reflects your spiritual and practical capabilities. Then grace will strengthen you to advance behind enemy lines.

---

[23] Job 8:7

*Creative planning*
Necessity, the saying goes, is the mother of invention. The challenge with operating under cover is that you need to become very creative in your planning and actions.

This is where you have to rely on the Spirit of God in you to give you fresh insight and new solutions that will promote you in the marketplace.

Creativity is our birthright as believers. But sadly many people seem to shut down their brains in the name of obedient Christianity.

While most Christians have a value for wisdom, most do not have an equal value for the role of creativity in their God-given responsibilities. This is because Creativity often involves doing something new, breaking new frontiers and doing something unusual.

This challenges the status quo already embedded in most minds. Yet it is creativity that illustrates the presence of wisdom: *"Wisdom is vindicated by all her children."*[24]

One of the most natural parts of being created in the image of God is the ability to dream and dream big. It's a God-given gift. Yet many believers, in their perverse attempts to please God, kill the very capacity He gave them.

Believers should be the most creative individuals on earth. We, after all, have the mind of Christ. Operating behind enemy lines tests your creative capability to the limit.

When unbelievers lead the way in inventions and artistic expressions; it is because the church has embraced a false kind of spirituality.[25]

---

[24] Luke7:35
[25] Bill Johnson, *Dreaming with God: Co-Laboring with God for Cultural Transformation*

*Dynamic decision-making*
Sometimes it feels like many believers live in a bubble that does not reflect the real world. Operating behind enemy lines requires speedy decision making amongst lots of competing choices. Time is a luxury that cannot be afforded in these environments.

We make decisions in increasingly complex, high-risk, and dynamic environments that evolve over time in unpredictable ways, and the options that we have available in our daily decisions have exponentially increased.

For example, when shopping in a store the item diversity on the shelves are large, menus in the restaurants offer a large variety, books to select from in the bookstore are large, etc. We are living a choice explosion era. This is where dynamic decision making becomes necessary.

Some make decisions only after getting all the facts. But what happens when all the facts are not available. How about eighty percent of the facts?

By definition, dynamic decision-making is interdependent decision-making that takes place in an environment that changes over time either due to the previous actions of the decision maker or due to events that are outside of the control of the decision maker.[26]

In this sense, dynamic decisions, unlike simple and conventional one-time decisions, are typically more complex and occur in real-time and involve more parameters that you cannot always control.

These are fast-paced decisions made sometimes with opaque or incomplete information. You have to be able to trust your instinct in this scenario. Believers need to develop a trust in their intuition

---

[26] https://en.wikipedia.org/wiki/Dynamic_decision-making

based on a strong knowledge of the Word of God to make this possible.

*Effective evidence and administration*
As the Church of Christ, we need to base all our practical decisions on the best evidence possible. This requires us to understand the reasoning behind decisions and positions taken by players in the marketplace. How do we obtain this vital intelligence except we go behind enemy lines.

It is not good enough merely living with a Kingdom mentality, which creates a renewed mind. The renewed mind should understand that the King's dominion must be realized at all levels of society for an effective witness to take place. This will require believers to engage with and operate behind enemy lines to be able to impact at the highest levels.

So enough of this timid, ineffective, self-pitying and weak Christianity. Getting saved is not a destination; it is a passport to a new journey as a Kingdom citizen to rule and reign on the earth.

*Knowledge, research and preparation*
Skill acquisition will be key in the last days for the Church. We must be able to speak the language of the marketplace.

It is time we put off the cloak of inactivity and complacency. At some point, we must go beyond being simply "sinners saved by grace." As we learn to live from our new position in Christ, we will bring forth the greatest exploits of all time. No more timid Christianity.

As evident in the bible, David needed more than the anointing to lead. He also needed skill. And that starts with knowledge acquisition and adequate preparation.

*"So he fed them according to the integrity of his heart; and guided them by the **skilfulness** of his hands."*[27]

---

[27] Psalm 78:72

# CHAPTER FOUR

## Spiritual Keys to Operating Behind Enemy Lines

Developing essential skills to successfully operate in the marketplace is possible; don't despair, God's people. God already has his people positioned and He is still planting more.

God will never leave himself without a witness in any generation. The question today is this: Can you operate behind the enemy lines? Do you have what it takes? Are you yielded enough to God for Him to use you?

It is settled in scriptures that God will use our marketplace engagement not only to transfer the wealth of the wicked but also to make the kingdoms of this world become His. God is in the business of using vocational skills to take over the mountains.

*"Then I lifted up my eyes and looked, and behold, there were four horns. So I said to the angel who was speaking with me, "What are these?" And he answered me, "These are the horns which have scattered Judah, Israel and Jerusalem." Then the Lord showed me four craftsmen. I said, "What are these coming to do?" And he said, "These are the horns which have scattered Judah so that no man lifts up his head; but these **craftsmen have come to terrify them,** to throw down the horns of the nations who have lifted up their horns against the land of Judah in order to scatter it."[28]*

This is one of the most alarming passages in the Bible. Not because it deals with spiritual warfare, but because

---

[28] Zechariah 1:18-21 NASB

God's tools for victory are not common knowledge for most of us today. In these verses, the people of God were being terrorised and scattered by abusive authorities and powers (Horns). Hopelessness was the theme of the day, and the confidence that God was with them was at an all time low.

The God of all wisdom illumines a truth that is to awaken the people of God to His end-time plans. He sends forth His army to tear down the military strongholds. Who are His soldiers? CRAFTSMEN! (Business folks)

Not since God first sent a choir into war has there been such an outlandish strategy for battle. This is a plan that only Wisdom could design.

The four craftsmen were God's answer to the four horns that had attempted to scatter His people. Those committed to skilful wisdom (artistic expression) will dismantle the strongholds of abusive power.

Craftsmen are not simply woodworkers and painters. Nor does that title belong only to actors and musicians. Everyone, doing their God-given task with excellence, creativity, and integrity is a craftsman in the biblical sense. The opposition that surrounds us seems great, but it cannot stand against the demonstration of God's people wielding this great weapon of war.

The Bible tells us that in the last days the nations will come to His holy nation asking us to teach them the Word of the Lord (see Micah 4:1-2).

Is it possible that this is their response to seeing us filled with the Spirit until His wisdom is on display? I think so. The wisdom of God will again be reflected in His people. The Church, which is presently despised, will again be reverenced and admired. The Church will again be a praise in the earth (see Jer. 33:9). But we must learn to use our activities in the marketplace to glorify God. Being undercover in the marketplace is doable because it is possible to have contact without contamination. After all, Samuel grew up in the same house as the sons of Eli, yet he was not contaminated by their evil ways.

As previously stated and it is worth repeating; throughout much of church history, people have been stripped of their God-given gifts, talents, and desires under the guise of devotion and consecration to Christ. This stripped-down version of Christianity removes the believer from ministry, and relegates that privilege to a certain class of Christians called "ministers."

The regular believer's role is reduced to mere financial and emotional support of those in public ministry. And of course to serve as workers in the "local church."

The honour of service and giving to promote ministry must not be devalued, but its emphasis should never be at the expense of each individual carrying their own creative expression of the Gospel through realising their God-given dreams and desires. This is the Kingdom paradigm needed to embrace operating in the marketplace.

In this chapter, I want to give you some of the spiritual keys to thriving in enemy territories. However, you must develop self-awareness before engaging the marketplace.

You must know your strengths and of course your weak points. Pray for grace in your area of weakness and put practical countermeasures in place to support you. This way, you can have contact without contamination.

**NUMBER 1:** The first key is to *learn and know the ways of the enemy.*

Learn their ways, learn their language, know what they know, get skilled about them and earn their culture.

The Bible says in 2 Corinthians Chapter 2:11 that *'we are not ignorant of the devices of the devil'.* In other words, if we are not ignorant then we are knowledgeable. So if we don't know the devices of the devil, we won't know what to avoid.

Hence, we need to know their ways. You must possess skills in the area of your assignment. You must learn to know the ways of the enemy.

Moses was schooled in the ways of Egypt. Daniel was skilled in the ways of Babylon. You need to be skilled in related matters to earn credibility in the marketplace. So when it comes to blending behind enemy lines skill is needed. You have to have skill in the area you are supposed to be infiltrating.

You need to have skills that make you not to negatively stand out. So it's very important, absolutely important that you learn the ways of the enemy before you can dispose that enemy.

**NUMBER 2:** Key number two is to **Learn to become all things to all men but have your red lines.** Learn to become adaptive. In other words, become flexible but have your red lines in Christ. You must be able to have contact without contamination.

You need to become flexible. Learn to become as wise as a serpent. You need to have appropriate skills suitable for diverse temperaments.

Why must you stand out for the wrong reason? Example; If you are fasting and do not use mints to freshen your breath all day, you will stand out not because you are fasting, but because you did not step up your oral hygiene, hence your smelly breath. So you have failed the test of blending in. Behind enemy lines, it is wise not to draw unnecessary attention to yourself. Knowing how to both blend in and stand out as led by the Spirit of God is an essential spiritual skill to have in hostile territories. You have to learn to be all things to all men,. if you are to survive behind enemy lines. I have already tackled this point in earlier Chapters.

**NUMBER 3:** You need discipline and dedication. The third key is good **discipline and dedication through consecration.** In Daniel chapter1 verse 6 the Bible says, *'Daniel decided not to pollute himself with the portion of the King's food.* You need discipline.

What do I mean? Things you normally give up on, when you are behind the enemy lines, you need discipline and strength not to give up. Why? Because help may not come readily while under cover. Survival skill is essential for undercover agents. You must know how to improvise and endure situations you may not normally face.

If you are conducting a daytime reconnaissance by foot behind enemy lines and you are tired, you have to keep walking to stay alive. Because you can't just camp anywhere you like, you need dedication and endurance. You need to be focused on what you are doing.

You have to keep going and be tenacious regardless of how you feel. You have to learn to encourage yourself in the marketplace because behind enemy lines you can't afford to be discouraged.

In enemy territories there aren't people there to encourage you; hence you have to keep going. The Bible says we should *"be strengthened with might by Christ in our inner man..."*[29]

That's what happened to David in 1 Samuel chapter 30 when he got back to Ziklag. The Bible says he encouraged himself in the Lord. He realised that with no one available to do it, he had to learn to encourage himself. That is a vital trait to survive behind enemy lines.

You must learn that it's good to have friendship and fellowship, but if you don't know how to encourage yourself in the Lord, you are in trouble.
Because there are times when you will not believe the challenges you are facing and you have to learn to encourage yourself.

---

[29] Ephesians 3:16

You cannot survive behind enemy lines if you do not have spiritual stature. You need to grow where it matters. That is, in the spirit, in knowledge, in wisdom and in favour with God and man. So you need to grow and mature in the things of God before embarking on an undercover mission. Just like police do not send recruits on undercover missions but experienced officers, so it is with the kingdom of God. You need to be mature in the things of God to be able to prosper in enemy territories.

**NUMBER 4:** Confidence is the fourth key characteristic. **Confidence** is a vital key to thriving behind enemy lines. The Bible says, *"do not cast away your confidence..."*[30]

Confidence and being in character is essential. Talking about the story of Esther, she had to display confidence to maintain her cover in the palace.

---

[30] Hebrews 10:35

For a Jew to pretend not to be a Jew requires acting skills and confidence. Any mistake could have led to her death in the palace. But she stayed in character and maintained confidence behind enemy lines. Confidence gives you believability and authenticity in the marketplace. So to succeed behind enemy lines, you need confidence.

**NUMBER 5:** The fifth key is that you must **know who and whose you are.** You cannot afford to lose your identity in the enemy's territory, otherwise you are dead.

You must adapt but you must still know whose you are. You are under cover but you are not lawless. You are under cover but you must have your red lines. I mean, if you know the rules that govern being under cover, you know, for example, you are allowed to do certain things but there are certain things you can't do.

You have to constantly remind yourself of your mission and who you are working for while still in character under cover. If you lose yourself you will lose your mission. You must learn to blend in to a point but you also must know where the red line is. So it is very important, for you to maintain the balance.

**NUMBER 6:** Supersensitivity to God's voice and the Holy Spirit. The sixth key is that you must **become Supersensitive to God's voice and the leading of His Spirit.**

Communication from the enemy camp must be coded so the enemy cannot pick it up, hence you have to have sensitivity and discretion. You have to be able to communicate back to base when undercover using all manner of tools and techniques.

But communication while under cover has to be a two-way thing. You must be able to receive new intelligence and instructions while operating in hostile territories. The voice of the Spirit of God is the greatest asset to a believer's destiny.

More importantly, you must be prepared to obey instructions that appear foolish. God's wisdom will direct you. He will ensure your survive and thrive without compromising. God will give you instructions that appear senseless but through the foolish things, He has promised to confound the wise.

So being sensitive to the leadings of the Spirit is essential. While operating in the marketplace, all your skills and desires will be tested to the fullest. You need to be able to obey instructions that are very peculiar to your situation. You have to learn to focus only on God and not on tradition or opinions of men.

So when you are operating behind the enemy lines you need sensitivity to hear the voice of God. You need absolute sensitivity to know when to break your cover and when not to break your cover; it's absolutely important.

So sensitivity to the voice of the Spirit is very important. Be ready for the instruction to come out from the master. The time will come when you will show your true colour, where you will show your true picture, be certain to know when that time is, because from the moment you are unveiled, that's it.

You can't go back behind enemy lines in that particular scenario again. So the moment you are out, that's it. Joseph of Arimathea could no longer be a follower in secret after that event but he waited for that event to fulfil scripture. It's very important that we understand this.

**NUMBER 7:** To prosper behind enemy lines, you must **operate in the fear of God.** The fear of God is key to operate in the marketplace and win with wisdom. It is not of God unless it is winning by righteousness.

Joseph revealed his secret of success in Egypt in Genesis chapter 42 verse 18 and he explained that it is the fear of God. The fear of God can be learned, as you can see in Deuteronomy chapter 4 verse 10. Solomon's final submission in Ecclesiastes chapter 12 verse 13, says, *'fear God and keep his commandment that is the summation of all things'*.

In Psalm 34 verse 9, we can see that the fear of God leads to prosperity. The Bible says, there is no want to those who fear him. The main Hebrew and Greek words translated fear in the Bible can have several shades of meaning, but in the context of the fear of the Lord, they convey a positive reverence. The Hebrew verb *yare* can mean "to fear, to respect, to reverence" and the Hebrew noun *yirah* "usually refers to the fear of God and is viewed as a positive quality.

This fear acknowledges God's good intentions (Ex. 20:20). ... This fear is produced by God's Word (Ps. 119:38; Prov. 2:5) and makes a person receptive to wisdom and knowledge (Prov. 1:7; 9:10)."[31] The Greek noun *phobos* can mean "reverential fear" of God, "not a mere 'fear' of His power and righteous retribution, but a wholesome dread of displeasing Him."[32]

This is the type of positive, productive fear Luke describes in the early New Testament Church and this is the fear that is needed to thrive behind enemy lines.

---

[31] Warren Baker and Eugene Carpenter, *The Complete Word Study Dictionary: Old Testament*, 2003, pp. 470-471
[32] Vine's Complete Expository Dictionary of Old and New Testament Words, 1985, *"Fear, Fearful, Fearfulness"*

So, rather than a paralysing terror, the positive fear of the Lord taught in the Bible is a key element in effecting change and keeping our red lines in the marketplace. It helps us have a proper, humble perspective of ourselves in relation to our awesome God; it helps us in times of temptation when we need to remember the serious consequences of disobeying God; and it motivates us to become more like our loving Creator.

I hope these few strategies will help you see that we are in the world but not of the world. We are supposed to be operating behind enemy lines guided by the wisdom of God.

**NUMBER 8:** To prosper behind enemy lines, you need to **have a Mentor.** This will be a person who has the spiritual capacity to guide and deal with principalities that may be proving tough for you. Knowledge without the pain of discovery is what mentors provide.

Mentors can also give you spiritual cover to ease your days behind enemy lines. Who you are connected to spiritually speaking can determine your capacity to gain certain advantages in the marketplace. Connect rightly, it can be the difference in your battle to reclaim your inheritance in the marketplace. Where will Samuel be without Eli, Joshua without Moses or Elisha without Elijah? We all need the input of mentors in this battle space. When you find an uncommon mentor, do all you can to keep him or her. Pay the price to stay in the company of greatness.

**NUMBER 9:** To prosper behind enemy lines, you need to **be a person of Prayer.** You have to birth all the things discussed above in the place of prayer. You have to pray into your flesh what Christ has already delivered for you.

You have to obtain heaven's verdict on every issue and then birth it in the place of prayer. This will shield you as you war behind enemy lines. It will keep you accurate and spot on regarding God's will in every situation. If you get prayer right you will get everything else right. You will be able to bring into existence visions, insights and revelations God has shown you.

# CHAPTER FIVE

## Divine Guidance is Essential to Reclaiming the Marketplace

God created man to have dominion over all the earth. Dominion speaks of Kingdom or domain. Man lost it at Eden, but in Christ, the Dominion or Rulership of the Kingdom is restored back to man.

*"Until John the Baptist began to preach, the laws of Moses and the messages of the prophets were your guides. But now the Good News of the Kingdom of God is preached, and eager multitudes are forcing their way in. 17But that doesn't mean that the law has lost its force in even the smallest point. It is stronger and*

103

*more permanent than heaven and earth."*[33]

Up until John the Baptist, the Law of Moses was fully operational. The people also had the books of the prophets (all announcing the coming of the King, the Messiah).

The first five books of the Bible are known as the "Pentateuch" or the "Books of Moses" these are:

- Genesis – Creation, the fall, sin, how Israel came to be a nation and then came to be in Egypt.
- Exodus – The deliverance of the people of Israel from slavery in Egypt.
- Leviticus – The book of the law.
- Numbers – The wandering in the wilderness.
- Deuteronomy – Israel preparing to move into the Promised Land.

---

[33] Luke 16

After the books of the Law (the first 5 books of the bible), from Joshua to Malachi are the books of the prophetic writings). They all spoke about Jesus. The Master confirms this Himself on the Road to Emmaus:

*"Now behold, two of them were travelling that same day to a village called Emmaus, which was seven miles from Jerusalem. And they talked together of all these things which had happened. So it was, while they conversed and reasoned, that Jesus Himself drew near and went with them. But their eyes were restrained, so that they did not know Him.*

*And He said to them, "What kind of conversation is this that you have with one another as you walk and are sad?" Then the one whose name was Cleopas answered and said to Him, "Are You the only stranger in Jerusalem, and have You not known the things which happened there in these days?"*

*And He said to them, "What things?" So they said to Him, "The things concerning Jesus of Nazareth, who was a Prophet mighty in deed and word before God and all the people, and how the chief priests and our rulers delivered Him to be condemned to death, and crucified Him. But we were hoping that it was He who was going to redeem Israel. Indeed, besides all this, today is the third day since these things happened. Yes, and certain women of our company, who arrived at the tomb early, astonished us. When they did not find His body, they came saying that they had also seen a vision of angels who said He was alive. And certain of those who were with us went to the tomb and found it just as the women had said; but Him they did not see." Then He said to them, "O foolish ones, and slow of heart to believe in all that the prophets have spoken! Ought not the Christ to have suffered these things and to enter into His glory?" And beginning at Moses and all the Prophets,*

*He expounded to them in all the Scriptures the things concerning Himself."*[34]

Christ is the theme of the entire revelation of God's word. He is promised in Genesis, revealed in the law, prefigured in its history, praised in its poetry, proclaimed in its prophecy, provided in its Gospels, proved in its Acts, pre-eminent in its Epistles and prevailing in Revelation.

He is seen in every verse and every book of the Bible. In many types and shadows Christ was revealed in the Old Testament.

In all cases, more than one representation of Him exists in each book; but let's take a look at a typical depiction of Christ in the Bible. It's a matter of personal revelation.

---

[34] Luke 24:13-27

### Change of Barton

*"Let your light so shine before men, that they may see your good works and glorify your Father in heaven. 17 "Do not think that I came to destroy the Law or the Prophets. I did not come to destroy but to fulfill. 18For assuredly, I say to you, till heaven and earth pass away, one jot or one tittle will by no means pass from the law till all is fulfilled."35*

*"Then He said to them, "These are the words which I spoke to you while I was still with you, that all things must be fulfilled which were written in the Law of Moses and the Prophets and the Psalms concerning Me."36*

After his temptations in the wilderness and at the start of His ministry Jesus declared:

---

35 Matthew 5:16-17
36 Luke 24:44

*"From that time Jesus began to preach and to say, "Repent, for the kingdom of heaven is at hand."*[37]

*"But He said to them, "I must preach the kingdom of God to the other cities also, because for this purpose I have been sent."*[38]

And to finally confirm this, Jesus took three of his disciples to witness a handover ceremony:

*"Now after six days Jesus took Peter, James, and John his brother, led them up on a high mountain by themselves; 2and He was transfigured before them. His face shone like the sun, and His clothes became as white as the light. 3And behold, Moses and Elijah appeared to them, talking with Him. 4Then Peter answered and said to Jesus, "Lord, it is good for us to be here; if You wish, let us*

---

[37] Matthew 4:17
[38] Luke 4:43

make here three tabernacles: one for You, one for Moses, and one for Elijah."

*⁵While he was still speaking, (God shut him and his religious spirit up) behold, a bright cloud overshadowed them; and suddenly a voice came out of the cloud, saying, "This is My beloved Son, in whom I am well pleased. Hear Him!" ⁶And when the disciples heard it, they fell on their faces and were greatly afraid. ⁷But Jesus came and touched them and said, "Arise, and do not be afraid." ⁸When they had lifted up their eyes, they saw no one but Jesus only. (the Law and the prophet were gone). ⁹Now as they came down from the mountain, Jesus commanded them, saying, "Tell the vision to no one until the Son of Man is risen from the dead." ¹⁰And His disciples asked Him, saying, "Why then do the scribes say that Elijah must come first?"*

*¹¹Jesus answered and said to them, "Indeed, Elijah is coming first and will restore all things. ¹²But I say to you that Elijah has come already, and they did not know him but did to him whatever they wished. Likewise the Son of Man is also about to suffer at their hands." 13Then the disciples understood that He spoke to them of John the Baptist."39*

*Key points to note:*

1) This meeting on the mountain was not all about transfiguration; it was also about Transferring.
2) Jesus as it were "picked up the Barton" from Moses (the Law) and Elijah (The Prophets). Luke 16 [NLT] - 16*"Until John the Baptist began to preach, the laws of Moses and the messages of the prophets were your guides. But now the Good News of the Kingdom of God is preached,*
3) The conversation on the mount between Moses, Elijah and Jesus was about the closure of an assignment and the start of a new one, (the gospel of the kingdom).

---

[39] Mathew 17:1-13

4) Peter had a religious spirit, which afflicts many churches today. He wanted to build monuments to the dead. Many of us are busy building monuments for the dead. God is not in it.

5) After the Voice came from heaven that confirmed the transfer that just took place, when the disciples looked, it was only Jesus that remained. Now the Law and the Prophets have had their day. Jesus is the only one we must now preach.

6) Before John the Baptist all that could be preached was the Law and the Prophets, but when Jesus came the prophecies and the law were fulfilled under a new grace of God.

John 1:45- *Philip found Nathanael and said to him, "We have found Him of whom Moses in the law, and also the prophets, wrote--Jesus of Nazareth, the son of Joseph."*

Romans 3:21- *But now the righteousness of God apart from the law is revealed, being witnessed by the Law and the Prophets.*

We are henceforth mandated to preach only the gospel of the Kingdom and reign on earth like kings exercising Authority and Dominion over all things. Jesus then conferred on us the kingship of this Kingdom:

Let us read some more scriptures.
*"But the saints of the Most High will receive the kingdom and will possess it forever-yes, for ever and ever."*[40]

*"And I bestow upon you a kingdom, just as My Father bestowed one upon Me, [30]that you may eat and drink at My table in My kingdom, and sit on thrones judging the twelve tribes of Israel."*[41]

---

[40] Daniel 7:18 - 18
[41] Luke 22:29 – 29

*"Do not fear, little flock, for it is your Father's good pleasure to give you the kingdom."*[42]

A Kingdom is a Governing Authority that influences its territories. If we understand what the kingdom is, we will then be able to understand who the Kings of the kingdom should be and the Keys with which to enter the Kingdom. Our job is to reclaim the marketplace. For some of us, we will do so by being overtly Christian so much so that from a mile away, everybody will recognise that fact.

But for others, there will be a need to operate quietly behind enemy lines to fully study the enemy and rise through their ranks before unveiling ourselves as agents of the only true Jehovah.

Kingdom of Heaven is A PLACE (which we can experience on the earth); while

---

[42] Luke 12:32- 32

the Kingdom of God is GOD'S WAY OF DOING THINGS. HIS VALUES, HIS PRINCIPLES—THEREFORE HIS WORD.

The Word of God is still the final authority in all things.

*"From that time Jesus began to preach and to say, "Repent, for the kingdom of heaven is at hand."*[43]

*"But He said to them, "I must preach the kingdom of God to the other cities also, because for this purpose I have been sent."*[44]

So Jesus came to preach the Kingdom of God so that we can be ready to receive and enter the Kingdom of Heaven. You have no business with the kingdom of heaven if you do not live your life in the kingdom of God.

---

[43] Matthew 4 – 17
[44] Luke 4 – 43

How can people live in heaven when they do not know God's ways of doing things? The Kingdom of God is revealed in the WORD of God. Obeying the word of God establishes the Kingdom of God in you. OBEDIENCE TO THE WORD OF GOD IS THE KEY TO RULERSHIP IN GOD'S KINGDOM on Earth.

*Divine guidance is key to reclaim the marketplace*
Recognizing the voice of the Holy Spirit is the greatest asset to any believer's destiny.

*"The LORD is my shepherd; I shall not want. 2He makes me to lie down in green pastures; He leads me beside the still waters. 3He restores my soul; He leads me in the paths of righteousness For His name's sake. 4Yea, though I walk through the valley of the shadow of death, I will fear no evil; For You are with me; Your rod and Your staff, they comfort me. 5You prepare a table before me in the presence*

*of my enemies; You anoint my head with oil; My cup runs over. ⁶Surely goodness and mercy shall follow me All the days of my life; And I will dwell in the house of the LORD Forever."*[45]

1. Divine Guidance commands DIVINE PROVISION. – Verse 1. Like Elijah in 1Kings 17.

2. Divine Guidance commands DIVINE REST. Vs 2-3. You will cease struggling, Hebrews 4:1-11. REST is an expression of Dominion.

3. Divine Guidance commands DIVINE CONFIDENCE. Vs 4A. Cast not away your confidence. Isaiah 30:15

4. Divine Guidance commands DIVINE CONQUEST. Vs 4B-5A. God shows you off. Conquest is where your mere presence disarms the enemy.

---

[45] Psalm 23:1-6

5. Divine Guidance commands DIVINE EMPOWERMENT. Vs 5B. Oil represents the anointing.

6. Divine Guidance commands DIVINE FAVOUR. Vs 6A.

7. Divine Guidance commands DIVINE SECURITY. Vs 6B

These are the seven instruments of Dominion & Breakthrough available to all the children of God to possess the mountains of culture of all nations.

These seven instruments should be present in your life as you embark on the mission to reclaim the marketplace for the Lord. You cannot survive under cover without these seven instruments of the Spirit of God.

Behind every supernatural exploit is divine guidance. The reality of God's power is manifested through obedience to Divine Direction.

Our provision and victory are at the place of obedience to God's voice.

*Invisible opportunities in difficult times*

The Sons of Issachar were able to understand the times and seasons so that they knew what Israel ought to do. Over the past few months, I have been contacted by more believers in serious financial difficulties than at any other period I can remember.

From Europe to America to Africa, the same is happening. I had to seek wisdom and clarity on what is going on.

Then I was shown a vision that not only explains what is going on but also the remedies. The kingdoms of this world are fighting back against the Kingdom of God as the hour draws near.

It is unwise for believers to rely purely on their acquired skills and knowledge to make it in the Marketplace.

Many of God's children have relied on acquiring more skills and education as a way out of poverty. But they forget that as God's children, they are operating in a world system that has been rigged against them.

The Bible says in 2 Timothy 3:7 - *"Ever learning, and never able to come to the knowledge of the truth".*

This means you can learn all you want and still not know the truth. So you can be well educated in error.

This is not a word against education. It simply means God cannot be found just in Education, but in His word. Don't confuse the two or mix them up. So because you are educated does not mean you know the Truth from the Word. With all your getting...get into the word.

Satan has set up the systems of this world to favour only those that serve him. So we cannot win the battle on Satan's terms or using his tools.

This means as the enemy fights back; believers need to build superior infrastructure in the spirit. You need to grow where it matters.

As I have said before, money always flows in the direction of spiritual power; either Godly or Satanic. You cannot control wealth of any tangible sum on the earth without possession of spiritual power.

Your skill and knowledge will not distinguish you as many believers already found out. The system of this world is not a fair one. The strong serves the weak. The educated serves the uneducated.

The seemingly knowledgeable work for those who seem unqualified. The scripture has already said that by strength shall no man prevail[46]. But many fail to take heed of this wisdom.
To succeed and dominate the financial devils on the earth, we must intensify our spiritual warfare and grow in the things of God.

Lukewarmness and mixture of two systems will kill all future opportunities. Decide this day who you will serve. If God, be resolute and refuse to compromise. Compromise always lead to captivity in the end.

Opportunity awaits, but the power of recognition is needed to see them. For in God, we see not through our eyes, but through what we know.

---

[46] 1 Samuel 2:9

You were born for dominion. You are the light of the world. Obedience to God's word and voice brings dominion and enablement to breakthrough all opposition in the Marketplace. Step out and become all that God wants you to be. God bless you.

# CHAPTER SIX

## The Distinguishing factor in the Marketplace

*"And you shall remember the Lord your God, for it is He who gives you **power to get wealth**, that He may establish His covenant which He swore to your fathers, as it is this day."*[47]

POWER is needed to get wealth, because; resistance is implied. You don't need power to obtain something if there is no resistance or contending force in place to prevent your getting it. Money flows in the direction of Spiritual Power (either Godly or Satanic); because money is controlled by evil spiritual forces.

---

[47] Deuteronomy 8:18

Money is not the same thing as Cash – It is what two people say it is. Money is whatever you have that is exchangeable for what you need... *and cash is the lowest form of money.* So the more Spiritual Power you have, the greater the flow of money in your direction.

*Egypt example.*
Egypt employed Spiritual Powers to keep the Children of Israel in bondage. That is why God had to first destroy all the gods of Egypt before Israel could be released. He could have killed the Pharaoh easily first, but that would not change anything as a new king would simply be crowned and the gods would still be in control.

But we see that as the gods of Egypt were destroyed, the gold and silver of Egypt were unlocked and released to the children of Israel. So money always follows whenever spiritual victory is secured. WHY? Because the spiritual always controls the Natural.

Money is controlled by spiritual forces. Money flows in the direction of spiritual power – The day spiritual forces/authority changed in Egypt; Money also followed it.

*Spiritual Power Controls the Marketplace.*

Luke.11:21-22 - *When a strong man, fully armed, guards his own palace, <u>his goods are in peace</u>. But when a stronger than he comes upon him and overcomes him, he takes from him all his armor in which he trusted, and divides his spoils.*

You must be able to bind the strongman before his spoils can be obtained in any land. Satan took control of the wealth of the world through Adam in the garden. But because Satan in NOT OMNIPRESENT, he appoints demons as commanders over Territories, nations and cities. These territorial spirits control the economies and marketplaces in all the earth.

So before you can successfully engage under cover and succeed in the marketplace as a believer, you have to contend with the evil spiritual forces controlling the wealth in that territory.

What happens in the **Natural** is controlled by happenings in the **Spiritual.** (What happens in the valley is determined by what is happening at the mountaintop. What Happens in the **Mountain-Top** (Place of Spiritual Encounter) affects the **outcomes in the Valley** (Marketplace)

Exodus 17: *⁸ Now Amalek came and fought with Israel in Rephidim. ⁹ And Moses said to Joshua, "Choose us some men and go out, fight with Amalek. Tomorrow I will stand on the top of the hill with the rod of God in my hand." ¹⁰ So Joshua did as Moses said to him, and fought with Amalek. And Moses, Aaron, and Hur went up to the top of the hill.* **¹¹ And so it was, when Moses held up his hand, that Israel prevailed; and**

***when he let down his hand, Amalek prevailed***. *12 But Moses' hands became heavy; so they took a stone and put it under him, and he sat on it. And Aaron and Hur supported his hands, one on one side, and the other on the other side; and his hands were steady until the going down of the sun. 13 So Joshua defeated Amalek and his people with the edge of the sword. 14 Then the Lord said to Moses, "Write this for a memorial in the book and recount it in the hearing of Joshua, that I will utterly blot out the remembrance of Amalek from under heaven." 15 And Moses built an altar and called its name, The-Lord-Is-My-Banner; 16 for he said, "Because the Lord has sworn: the Lord will have war with Amalek from generation to generation."*

Therefore, spiritual power controls wealth. Either Satanic spiritual power or God's spiritual power. So to become wealthy you have to be in one of the two camps (one is temporal, the other is permanent).

## UNDERSTANDING THE MARKETPLACE –
*Tyre and Sidon*

Ezek. 28: 1-16
*The word of the Lord came to me again, saying,* **2** *"Son of man, say to* **THE PRINCE OF TYRE***, 'Thus says the Lord God:*
*"Because your heart is lifted up, And you say, 'I am a god,  I sit in the seat of gods,  In the midst of the seas,'* **Yet you are a man, and not a god,** *Though you set your heart as the heart of a god;* **3** *(Behold, you are wiser than Daniel! There is no secret that can be hidden from you!* **4 With your wisdom and your understanding You have gained riches for yourself,  And gathered gold and silver into your treasuries;**
**5** *By your great wisdom in trade you have increased your riches,  And your heart is lifted up because of your riches),"* **6** *'Therefore thus says the Lord God:*
*"Because you have set your heart as the heart of a god,* **7** *Behold, therefore, I will*

*bring strangers against you, The most terrible of the nations; And they shall draw their swords against the beauty of your wisdom, And defile your splendor.*
**8** *They shall throw you down into the Pit, And you shall die the death of the slain In the midst of the seas.* **9** *"Will you still say before him who slays you, 'I am a god'? But you shall be a man, and not a god, In the hand of him who slays you.*
**10** *You shall die the death of the uncircumcised By the hand of aliens; For I have spoken," says the Lord God.'"*

**11** *Moreover the word of the Lord came to me, saying,* **12** *"Son of man, take up a lamentation for the king of Tyre, and say to him, 'Thus says the Lord God: "You were the seal of perfection, Full of wisdom and perfect in beauty.* **13** ***You were in Eden, the garden of God; Every precious stone was your covering:*** *The sardius, topaz, and diamond, Beryl, onyx, and jasper, Sapphire, turquoise, and emerald* *with gold. The workmanship of your timbrels and pipes Was prepared for you on the day you were created.* **14** *"You were the anointed cherub who covers; I established you; You were on the holy mountain of God; You walked back and forth in the midst of fiery stones.*

**15** **You were perfect in your ways from the day you were created, Till iniquity was found in you.** **16** *"By the abundance of your trading You became filled with violence within, And you sinned; Therefore I cast you as a profane thing Out of the mountain of God; And I destroyed you, O covering cherub, From the midst of the fiery stones.*

## *Key facts from this scripture passage*
- Prince of Tyre – A Human Being
- King of Tyre – Satan.
- But the Prince is controlled by the KING.

So we wrestle not against flesh and blood. When you operate in the marketplace, you must learn and know how to successfully speak to the King of Tyre while looking at the Prince of Tyre.

There are certain positions in Industry and Politics that you cannot attain unless you are part of an occult group. This is a global reality not just African. You need a superior power to overrule these enemies.

Jesus had spiritual power. He had Power over Territorial Spirits. *So he had power over material things as well.* Jesus demonstrated his mastery over the elements by asking Peter to cast his net over the other side.

Because He had taken control over the territory he could control the fish in the sea. Fish responded to the command of the Master. THE ELEMENTS WILL NOT RESPOND TO YOU UNTIL YOU DEVELOP SPIRITUAL STATURE.

**So what distinguishes you in the Marketplace as you operate under cover?**

- Not your Education
- Not your Contacts
- Not your Parents
- Not your Nationality or Race

IT IS <u>THE BLESSING</u> OF THE LORD!

Proverbs10:22 – *The BLESSING of the Lord, it maketh rich and adds no sorrow with it.*

Genesis28:4 - *...I give thee the BLESSING of Abraham....*

Deuteronomy 12:15 - *....According to the BLESSING of the Lord thy God, which He has given thee...*

Deuteronomy 28:8 – *The Lord shall command the BLESSING upon you...in your storehouses...*

Romans 15:29 – *And I'm sure that when I come unto you, I shall come in the fullness of the BLESSING of the gospel of Christ.*

# THE DISTINGUISHING FACTOR IN THE MARKETPLACE IS THE BLESSING OF GOD.

BLESSING simply means DIVINE EMPOWERMENT and AFFIRMATION.

The Blessing is primarily a spiritual occurrence – *But as the spirit controls the physical, there will be physical manifestations.* So Wealth and Prosperity, Good Health, Good family etc are not the BLESSING of God but consequences of having received the BLESSING.

Many try to define the wind by its results (moving branches). In the same way, we have wrongly tried to define the BLESSING of God by its results and consequences. The blessing of God can only be understood, defined, and appropriated by Focusing on its SOURCE and ESSENCE and not its results. The Blessing is the ability that God puts on you. It is the Super on your Natural

It is God's ability over your ability, so that you will have the ability of God. What happens if a person is financially rich without the blessing? – It will be subject to wealth transfer. If you are rich financially but dying of cancer; you are just a POOR man with Money.

If you are poor financially but in good health; You are just a Poor man with healthy body. THE BLESSING OF GOD brings Total Life Prosperity with nothing missing and nothing broken.   This is what sets you apart in the marketplace.

*HOW TO ACTIVATE THE BLESSING AS A BELIEVER.*
The Blessing of God is dependent on obedience to God's word and Divine Instruction.

**1.** OBEDIENCE TO DIVINE INSTRUCTIONS RELEASES THE BLESSING OF GOD.[48]

---

[48] Mat. 7:24

This allows the power of God to be made manifest in your life. You must obey divine instruction. Every disobedience to the Word moves you further away from your destiny of abundance in God. Obedience is our connector to the Promises of God.

**2.** WALK IN THE REALITIES OF THE COVENANT FOR WEALTH.

*"as long as the earth remaineth.... seedtime and harvest shall never cease."*[49]

Everything God created was from something (a seed). He created man from Himself He formed man from the clay. He commanded the ground to bring forth....

God always uses a SEED to produce the outcome (HARVEST) needed. Where is your seed? You must give God access to ALL you have before you can have access to All He has. If you want to enjoy God's

---

[49] Gen 8.22

Miracles you have to obey God's principles.

Obedience tells you where to go and how to get there. Covenant for Wealth tells you what to do when you get there to eat the good of the land. Finally; you have to learn to overrule yourself (your senses) before you can fully obey God. To do this you need to think the way heaven thinks.

So as I end this book, I want you to understand that the marketplace is governed by Satan and we need to reclaim it for the Lord. The blessing of the Lord empowers us but we need to know how to conduct ourselves behind enemy lines.

God bless you as you take your position in your allotted mountain. See you at the top.

# CHAPTER SEVEN

## *Wisdom is not Compromise*

As I end this book, one question could be agitating your mind. And that is: *Is this book not advocating compromise of our faith in an attempt to get to the top?*

Nothing could be far from the truth. As noted in Chapters three and four, you need to possess certain levels of spiritual maturity to work behind enemy lines. But in all these, you must separate tradition from scriptural instructions.

For instance, if you give a woman (not your wife) a kiss on the cheek to say goodbye (and some are offended), is that because you acted against scripture or is it tradition? Some will say that is sin, but there is no scriptural basis for that view.

Because something is culturally unacceptable to you does not make it unscriptural.

Many believers allow tradition to dictate their norms and then accuse those that do otherwise of compromise. You must be prepared to let go of tradition when operating under cover and allow the wisdom of God to direct you. You cannot survive behind enemy lines without God; hence your life must remain connected to God to make a success of it.

So in every situation you face in the marketplace, you have to keep asking a vital question: Is this Compromise or Wisdom?

This is where you have to allow yourself to be led by the Spirit of God. God wants all believers to possess the Spirit of wisdom. It is one thing to have the Holy Spirit inside you, but it is another thing to have the Holy Spirit flow as the Spirit of wisdom within you.

When God's wisdom prevails, there is no problem that cannot be solved. There is no daunting task that cannot be accomplished. God's wisdom surmounts them all. The Bible even says that the foolishness of God is wiser than the greatest wisdom of man! (1 Corinthians 1:25)

A person can be very well-educated and full of knowledge, but still lack wisdom. Still, Christians can be quite gullible. This is my main concern. That is why con artists love churches. I want to remind you again the same thing that our Lord said:

*"...I send you out as sheep in the midst of wolves. Therefore be wise as serpents and harmless as doves."*[50]

Be wise as serpents and harmless as doves. I don't have to teach on the last part. Being harmless comes easy to religious minds when operating in the

[50] Matthew 10:16

141

marketplace. But it is that "gentle" mind-set that makes believers easy targets for the enemy. There are many people in Christianity who are very trusting, but not discerning. Be wise as serpents. Don't let anyone think that you are a fool just because you are a believer.

After Jesus tells us to be wise as serpents and innocent as doves, two verses down He says:

*"You will be brought before governors and kings for My sake, as a testimony to them and to the Gentiles. But when they deliver you up, do not worry about how or what you should speak. For it will be given to you in that hour what you should speak; for it is not you who speak, but the Spirit of your Father who speaks in you."*[51]

Here, Jesus says that when you are brought before VIPs, governors and kings for His sake, do not worry about how or what you should speak because God will

---

[51] Matthew 10:18–20

give you the words to speak, *"for it is not you who speak, but the Spirit of your Father who speaks in you"*. Notice that He says that it is the *"Spirit of your Father"* who speaks in you. In other words, **wisdom is a Spirit.**

God told Moses: *"See, I have called by name Bezalel the son of Uri, the son of Hur, of the tribe of Judah. And I have filled him with the Spirit of God, in wisdom, in understanding, in knowledge, and in all manner of workmanship."*[52]

Paul prayed for the Ephesian church that God may give them *"the spirit of wisdom and revelation in the knowledge of Him."*[53]

And Joshua was *"full of the spirit of wisdom, for Moses had laid his hands on him."*[54]

---

[52] Exodus 31:2–3
[53] Ephesians 1:17
[54] Deuteronomy 34:9

Once you learn that wisdom is a spirit, ask God for wisdom every day and then learn to flow in the Spirit. Learn to walk in the Spirit of wisdom while operating behind enemy lines. Wisdom is not compromise. There are many sides to God. That is why His wisdom is called the "Manifold" wisdom.

Beloved, it really helps when God gives you *"a mouth and wisdom which all your adversaries will not be able to contradict or resist."*[55]

Wisdom is what you need to operate successfully behind enemy lines. The wisdom that only Christ gives. This will make you do things other believers may not fully understand or some will call compromise. But keep doing what wisdom directs you to do. This is essential to survive the pressure of the enemy.

---

[55] Luke 21:15

One time, the Pharisees asked Jesus, *"Should we pay taxes to Caesar?"* Their intention was to trap Jesus, and here is a paraphrase of what happened. If Jesus said, "No, you should not," they would accuse Him before Pontius Pilate of breaking the Roman law. If He said, "Yes, you should pay taxes to Caesar," they would say to him, "See, You are with them."

But Jesus, knowing what they were up to, said to them, *"Give Me a coin. Whose picture is on it?"* They all replied, "Caesar's."

*"Well, give to Caesar the things that are Caesar's and give to God the things that are God's,"* Jesus said. The Pharisees marvelled at His answer and kept silent. They could not catch Him in His words in the presence of the people.[56]

Beloved, God will give you a mouth and wisdom for every situation you encounter

---

[56] Luke 20:21–26

behind enemy lines. Just don't bother yourself with what other people will think or say. Whether it is what to say or what to do, Christ will give you the wisdom to handle the situation.

So ask God for the Spirit of wisdom to operate in you. Remember, one who is greater than Solomon—Jesus—is in you. He is the wisdom of God. He is at the Father's right hand and He is ready to become your wisdom in every crisis of your life, in every situation you face as your thrive behind enemy lines.

The Wisdom of God should become Rhema (received/spoken word) for you. Obeying that wisdom could look foolish, it could look dangerous, it could look like compromise. As long as the mouth of God has declared it, His zeal will definitely perform it.

*Finally*
This has been an interesting book to write because it could easily be

misunderstood as it deals with an unusual but necessary subject. This will fit in the category of matters Peter the Apostle would describe as *"hard to understand"* and which *"the untaught and unstable may twist to their own destruction."*

*"He speaks about these things in all his letters in which there are some matters that are **hard to understand**. The **untaught and unstable twist them to their own destruction,** as they also do with the rest of the Scriptures."*[57]

This also reminds me of David in the house of Saul. The Scriptures say:

*"So David went out wherever Saul sent him, and behaved wisely. And Saul set him over the men of war, and he was accepted in the sight of all the people and also in the sight of Saul's servants."*[58]

---

[57] 2 Peter 3:16 (HCSB)
[58] 1 Samuel 18:5 (NKJV)

David did not regard the call and anointing of God on him as a licence to be foolish. So for him to be accepted by all, a lot of human relational skill must have been required. Not too long ago, a friend told me of his experience at a conference and one of the break-out session speakers was a missionary in a predominantly Moslem country. He shared with the audience stories of a few Imams who have become followers of Christ but who still keep their "job" as Imams.

This was partly due to the fact that conversion to Christianity is punishable by death in that country, but also it has now become a job and not a spiritual role for them. These Imams secretly attend fellowship with the missionaries but still kept their day jobs as Imams but doing less teaching as they delegated more to their assistants. The speaker was asking for prayers so that they will have wisdom on how to handle the situation.

Even in the liberal Western Europe, the skills highlighted in the book will become more and more necessary as the resistance to the Gospel increases. How does one, for example, in the UK health care sector obey the LORD without breaking the regulations? You are not allowed to pray or share your faith with patients, even if they are Christians. And as explained in this book, under the guise of offering a sacrifice, Samuel anointed David in the house of Jesse.

So for those who are in the marketplace, walking behind enemy lines is already a reality. This book will become a needed reference tool for them to survive and thrive in the marketplace.

My calling is to disciple the champions of faith in the secular arena. Few years ago, the Lord said to me in a vision:
*"It is the dawn of a new season for you and there is a shift to move to the next level. The time has come to empower my people to reach confidently beyond the*

*walls of the Church into the structures of Babylon; to redeem not only the persons therein but also to impact the systems redemptively; for my glory is about to be revealed in the Marketplaces of the earth. This will herald My promise of wealth transfer and the end of the ages. And you my son will be a key player in this endeavour".*

This mandate now informs all I do daily. And the Lord has opened many doors of opportunity for me to practically experience life behind enemy lines. To indeed prove there can be contact without contamination, leaning on His grace and everlasting arm all the time.

So I want you to be encouraged child of God. We are at the cusp of a new era as God begins to take over the mountains using His secret and not so secret Apostles in the Marketplace. The mountains of God have become the garrison of the Philistines.[59] God wants

---

[59] 1 Samuel 13

His mountains back. Now let us get to work. Let God be true and every man a liar. God bless you as you thrive in the marketplace using the wisdom of God.

# Other Books by Dr Charles Omole

I.    Church, Its time to Fly -- Learning to fly on Eagles Wing.

II.   How to Avoid Getting Hurt in Church -- 13 Steps that will protect you and help create an atmosphere for breakthroughs.

III.  Must I go to Church -- 8 Reasons why you must attend Church.

IV.   Freedom from Condemnation -- Breaking free from the burden & weight of sin.

V.    I cannot serve a big God and remain small

VI.   How to start your own business

VII.  How to Make Godly Decisions

VIII. How to avoid financial collapse

IX.   Let Brotherly love continue: An insight into love and companionship.

X.    Breaking out of the debt trap

XI.   Common Causes of Unanswered Prayer.

XII.    How to Argue with God and Win -- Biblical strategies on getting God's attention for all your circumstances all of the time

XIII.   Avoiding Power Failure-- How to generate spiritual power for daily success and victorious living.

XIV.    How long should I continue to pray when I don't see an answer?

XV.     SUCCESS KILLERS: Seven Habits of Highly Ineffective Christians.

XVI.    The Financial Resource Handbook – UK Edition

XVII.   Divine Strategies for uncommon breakthroughs: Living in the Reality of the Supernatural:

XVIII.  Keys to Divine Success

XIX.    Wrong Thoughts, Wrong Emotion and Wrong Living

XX.     Secrets of Biblical Wealth Transfer

XXI.    Journey to Fulfilment

XXII.   Prosperity Unleashed – A Definitive Guide to Biblical Economics

XXIII.  No More Debt – Volume 1

XXIV.   Understanding Dominion

XXV.    Advancement

For more information about our ministry, world outreaches and a free catalogue of our materials, please write to:

*Winning Faith Outreach Ministries*
*151 Mackenzie Road, London. N7 8NF,*

www.charlesomole.com
Email: Info@CharlesOmole.com

# NOTES

www.ingramcontent.com/pod-product-compliance
Lightning Source LLC
Chambersburg PA
CBHW072012040426
42447CB00009B/1602